P9-CLH-195

HARRIS COUNTY PUBLIC LIBRARY

345.73 Her
Herda, D. J.
Furman v. Georgia : the
     death penalty case

                              $31.93
                       ocn314114450
Rev. ed.   08/05/2010

Furman v. Georgia

The Death Penalty Case, Revised Edition

Titles in the series

LANDMARK SUPREME COURT CASES

The Dred Scott Case: Slavery and Citizenship, Revised Edition
ISBN-13: 978-0-7660-3427-3

District of Columbia v. Heller: The Right to Bear Arms Case
ISBN-13: 978-0-7660-3430-3

Furman v. Georgia: The Death Penalty Case, Revised Edition
ISBN-13: 978-0-7660-3428-0

New York Times v. United States: National Security and Censorship, Revised Edition
ISBN-13: 978-0-7660-3429-7

Furman v. Georgia

The Death Penalty Case, Revised Edition

LANDMARK SUPREME COURT CASES

GOLD EDITION

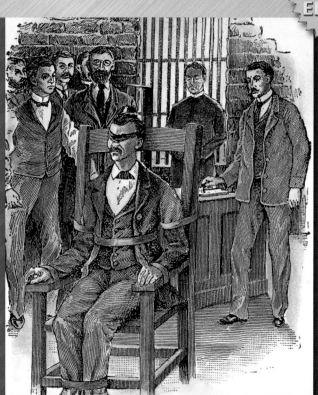

D. J. Herda

Enslow Publishers, Inc.
40 Industrial Road
Box 398
Berkeley Heights, NJ 07922
USA
http://www.enslow.com

Copyright © 2011 by D.J. Herda

All rights reserved.

No part of this book may be reproduced by any means
without the written permission of the publisher.

Library of Congress Cataloging-in-Publication Data

Herda, D. J., 1948–
    Furman v. Georgia : the death penalty case / D. J. Herda. — Rev. ed.
        p. cm. — (Landmark Supreme Court cases, gold ed.)
    Includes bibliographical references and index.
    Summary: "William Henry Furman was convicted of murder and sentenced
    to death after accidentally killing a resident of a home he was burglarizing.
    The constitutionality of the death penalty was challenged. This book examines
    the issues leading up to the case, the people involved in the case, and the
    present-day effects of the Court's decision"—Provided by publisher.
    ISBN 978-0-7660-3428-0
    1. Furman, William Henry—Trials, litigation, etc.—Juvenile literature. 2. Georgia—
    Trials, litigation, etc.—Juvenile literature. 3. Capital punishment—United States—
    Juvenile literature. 4. Capital punishment—Georgia—Juvenile literature. 5. Capital
    punishment. 6. Furman, William Henry—Trials, litigation, etc. I. Title.
    KF228.F87H47 2010
    345.73'0773—dc22

                                                          2009010107

Printed in the United States of America

022010 Lake Book Manufacturing, Inc., Melrose Park, IL

10 9 8 7 6 5 4 3 2 1

To Our Readers: We have done our best to make sure all Internet Addresses in this
book were active and appropriate when we went to press. However, the author
and the publisher have no control over and assume no liability for the material
available on those Internet sites or on other Web sites they may link to. Any
comments or suggestions can be sent by e-mail to comments@enslow.com or to
the address on the back cover.

♻ Enslow Publishers, Inc., is committed to printing our books on recycled paper.
The paper in every book contains 10% to 30% post-consumer waste (PCW). The
cover board on the outside of each book contains 100% PCW. Our goal is to do
our part to help young people and the environment too!

Illustration Credits: Associated Press/Wide World Photos, pp. 17, 19, 27, 30, 52, 75,
77, 80, 83, 101; Bureau of Justice Statistics, pp. 98, 99; Collection of the United
States Supreme Court, p. 64; The Granger Collection, New York, pp. 3, 14, 37;
National Archives, p. 58; Photos.com/Jupiterimages Corporation, p. 6; UPI
Photo/Eduardo Sverdin/Landov, p. 95; Wikipedia, p. 39.

Cover Illustration: Associated Press/ Wide World Photos.

Contents

The Furman case began with an attempted burglary in a Georgia home in 1967.

Georgia, 1967

CHAPTER 1

William Henry Furman, a twenty-six-year-old black man with a sixth-grade education, was not what most people called a bad man. He was, by his own admission, down on his luck. Recently laid off from his job, he bounced around his home state of Georgia for months. Everywhere he went he looked for a job, any job. He found his share of work, too, over the months, but none of the jobs were very good, and none were permanent. He went from gardener to dockworker, from janitor to delivery man. But no matter how hard he tried to get ahead, the jobs always ended too soon, and in time his money ran out.

Furman began showing signs of depression. He became sullen and moody. Eventually, hungry and broke, he turned to breaking and entering and to petty thievery to survive. Nothing major, according to Georgia State Patrol records.

A few things here, a few there. Mostly, he would look for a likely house and plan his assault well after dark, when the residents were either away or sure to be asleep. Then he would sneak in an open window or jimmy a locked door, rummage around for whatever valuables he could find, and be gone, usually within ten or fifteen minutes.

He had been caught a couple of times and each time was given a light or suspended sentence. He had been examined once by a state-appointed psychiatrist, who had found him to be emotionally disturbed and mentally impaired—but not enough to have him held in jail or committed to a mental institution. Usually he was back on the streets—and struggling to survive—within a matter of weeks.

Then on August 11, 1967, Furman's luck took a turn for the worse. He had just broken into the home of twenty-nine-year-old William Joseph Micke, Jr., the father of five young children. While Micke, his wife, and his children slept upstairs, Furman rifled through the lower level of the house for whatever valuables he could find.

Suddenly, around 2 A.M., Micke awoke to the sound of someone rummaging around downstairs. He crawled out of bed and made his way slowly toward the kitchen. The noises grew louder.

Furman, too, heard noises—the steadily approaching footsteps of William Micke. He pulled out the gun he had brought along with him—just in case he had to scare someone away. He paused and listened to the footsteps. Closer and closer they came. Not wanting to risk a confrontation, Furman turned and fled through the back door leading to the porch. As he ran, he tripped over an exposed washing machine cord and fell face-first against the hardwood floor. The gun discharged. The stray bullet pierced the back door. On the other side, Micke slumped slowly to the floor. William Joseph Micke was dead.

The police responded to the call quickly, and within minutes they had apprehended Furman just down the street from the scene of the crime. The murder weapon was still in his pocket. When his trial came up, Furman, on the advice of his court-appointed attorney, pleaded not guilty by reason of insanity. The courts ordered a psychiatric test, and the physicians who examined him agreed unanimously that he was mentally deficient. In their report they concluded that Furman experienced mild-to-moderate psychotic episodes associated with convulsive disorder.

The physicians testified in court that Furman was not psychotic at the time of his examination, but they agreed that he was not capable of cooperating with his defense attorney in the preparation of his own case. They concluded that he was in need of further psychiatric hospitalization and treatment.

Several days later, the superintendent of Georgia's Central State Hospital, where Furman had been committed while awaiting trial, revised his own earlier medical opinion after finding that Furman was "not psychotic at present, knows right from wrong, and is able to cooperate with his counsel in preparing his defense."[1] The court then ruled that William Henry Furman was competent to stand trial for murder in Chatham County Superior Court. Although the killing of Micke had been accidental, or at least committed without any intent to kill, Georgia state law at the time authorized that the death penalty be given whenever a murder took place during the commission of a felony, a class of crimes that includes burglary. Furman was tried, convicted, and scheduled for sentencing. Faced with imposing either life imprisonment or death on Furman, the jury chose death.

William Furman's attorneys were shocked. Their client was a man whom society had literally forgotten. He had seemed genuinely sorry for Micke's death. He had been down on his luck. He had turned to burglary only as a last-ditch effort to survive—while quite possibly being plagued by psychotic bouts.

But William Furman had one other thing going against him. He was black. And Georgia crime statistics showed that like most blacks found guilty of committing murder in that state during the sixties and seventies, that fact alone was reason enough to sentence him to death.

There were still various legal avenues open to Furman and his attorneys before the death sentence was carried out. There were motions to be filed. There were appeals to be made. And if it came right down to it, there was one last road to take. There was the Supreme Court of the United States.

Capital Punishment in America

Nearly six hundred inmates sat on death row in America's prisons at the time Furman was convicted of murder. They sat and they waited for someone to come and tell them their appeals had run out. They sat and they waited—thinking and hoping and praying, most likely—until someone arrived to pull the switch.

Of those death row inmates, several were teenagers, more than twenty were women, and a disproportionate number were blacks (329 blacks, 257 whites, and 14 identified as Puerto Rican, Chicano, or Native American). Yet no one had previously made a serious challenge to the death penalty based on the grounds that it discriminated against the nation's poor and oppressed.

The death penalty, or capital punishment, has been a common ingredient in America's judicial system since the system's Anglo-Saxon beginnings. Capital punishment had existed in Plymouth Colony and throughout much of New England since the early 1600s. It has existed throughout most of America ever since.

The death penalty in early America was usually the result of a criminal conviction for murder. But capital punishment was also handed out for a variety of other crimes. As many as eighteen different capital crimes existed on the law books of colonial America, depending upon the individual colony. In some colonies so many offenses were punishable by death that it seemed few other punishments existed.

As in England—on whose judicial system the American colonies based their own—and much of the rest of Europe, capital punishment was often handed out unpredictably and without just cause. In the American colony of Salem Village in 1692, three young girls triggered a rash of witchcraft trials that would eventually rock the colonies to their very core. The girls, who later admitted they were just having fun, accused a neighbor of practicing witchery, thus spurring a frantic search for witches, warlocks, and other demons. By the time the witch hunt was over, twenty people had been put to death. Nineteen "witches" had been hanged, and the husband of one woman convicted of being a witch had been crushed beneath a pile of stones for refusing to take part in the trials.

The panic that swept New England during the Salem Witch Trials was fueled by Cotton Mather, a well-known and influential clergyman, and other church and civic officials. These clerics used the trials to frighten their parishioners into becoming better Christians. Later, America's framers of the Constitution met to draft a new set of laws for a young nation. They recalled with horror the dangers of a church-influenced civil government, under which people could be put to death on the mere suggestion of wrongdoing and no separation of church and state or balance of powers existed.

To prevent a recurrence of such an event, the framers of the United States Constitution drafted the Eighth Amendment. This was one of the original ten amendments known as the Bill of Rights. It was adopted by Congress in 1791. The Eighth Amendment guarantees that anyone charged with or convicted of committing a crime shall be entitled to fair and equal treatment under the law. It reads, "Excessive bail shall not be required, nor excessive fines imposed, nor cruel and unusual punishments inflicted."

The Eighth Amendment has been interpreted over the years to prohibit torture, unnecessary cruelty, and any means of execution that might result in a prolonged and painful death. While the amendment did not specify whether or not execution itself could be considered "cruel and unusual punishment," various challenges to the death penalty have been made over the years based upon differing interpretations of this amendment.

Reverend George Burroughs was accused of witchcraft and hanged in Salem, Massachusetts, in 1692.

Some eighty years after the Eighth Amendment was passed into law, the Fourteenth Amendment was added to the Constitution. It reads:

> All persons born or naturalized in the United States, and subject to the jurisdiction thereof, are citizens of the United States and of the State wherein they reside. No State shall make or enforce any law which shall abridge the privileges or immunities of citizens of the United States; nor shall any State deprive any person of life, liberty or property, without due process of law; nor deny to any person within its jurisdiction the equal protection of the laws.

Armed with such sweeping protections for individual rights, many citizens' groups over the years have mounted campaigns aimed at abolishing capital punishment in the United States. Most of these groups have based their objections to capital punishment on the Eighth and Fourteenth Amendments, although some religious groups have objected solely on the grounds of the biblical fifth commandment, which states, "Thou shalt not kill."

These groups have argued that the government does not have the right to take a human life. They have produced various statistics showing that capital punishment rarely accomplishes its goal of discouraging others from committing capital crimes.

While these groups have not yet reached their ultimate goal of eliminating capital punishment in the United States, they *have* succeeded in influencing state governments to reduce the number of death penalties handed out.

During the half century from 1930 to 1987, nearly four thousand executions were conducted under state or federal authority. Throughout that period, though, increasing opposition to capital punishment had a marked effect on the steadily decreasing death rate from executions.

During the 1930s, there were 1,690 civil executions. During the 1940s, there were 1,284 executions. During the 1950s, there were 717. And from 1960 to 1969, there were only 191 civil executions. Another notable trend regarding capital punishment over the years is the way the carrying out of executions has been made more humane. In primitive and medieval societies, executions were often brutal affairs, designed as much to scare innocent citizens into obeying the laws of the state as they were to punish the offender. Burning, crucifixion, whipping, shooting, strangling, stoning, and boiling in oil—most often carried out in public—were all once common.

Today, the majority of executions involve the use of lethal injection, although some states use as alternative methods lethal gas, electrocution, hanging, and shooting by a firing squad. Although this last method is rarely used today, Gary Mark Gilmore was executed by firing squad on January 17, 1977. He had been convicted of the execution-type slaying of a young college student working as a motel manager in Provo, Utah.

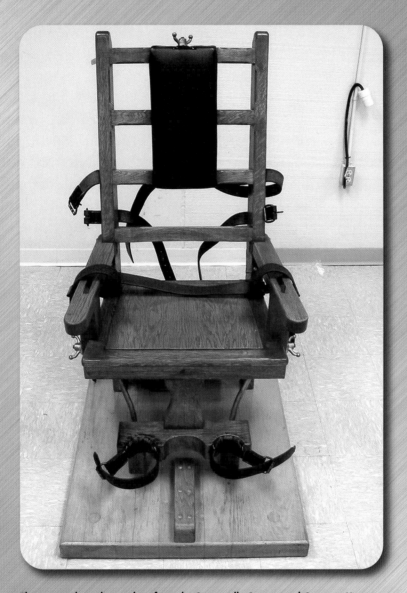

This is a modern electric chair from the Greensville Correctional Center in Virginia. Electrocution is no longer the main method used to carry out executions in this country. Most condemned murderers die by lethal injection.

By far, most felons sentenced to death have been executed for having committed murder, outnumbering the next largest category—rape—by nearly eight to one. (In *Coker* v. *Georgia*, 1977, the Court placed restrictions upon the use of the death penalty depending upon the types of crimes committed and the conditions under which the crimes were committed.) Other executions have been carried out as a result of convictions for crimes ranging from armed robbery and kidnapping to aggravated assault and espionage. Except in rare court-ordered instances, all executions take place in private.

Despite the apparent authority the United States Constitution gives the states to carry out the death penalty, thirteen states and the District of Columbia have never executed anyone, regardless of the nature or severity of the crime committed. A fourteenth state, Michigan, had embraced the death penalty until reversing its action in 1846—the only state ever to first enact and then ban the death penalty. As of April 1, 2009, Texas leads the nation in executions since 1976, with more than four hundred.[1]

Besides the obvious question of whether or not the government has the right to take a human life, opposition to capital punishment in America has for the most part revolved around three broad questions: Does capital punishment work to deter crime? Is it a violation of the Eighth and Fourteenth Amendments? And is it used fairly with regard to race?

This last question is the one that is easiest to answer in terms of statistics. African Americans throughout

A demonstrator carries a sign while wearing a box on his head with Florida Governor Jeb Bush's picture on it on March 5, 2001. The demonstration was organized as a protest against Florida's death penalty.

history have been shown to be greater targets of capital punishment than whites, in relation to both the general population and the population of America's prisons. African Americans represented 53 percent of all prisoners executed between 1930 and 1987; whites, only 46 percent.

Not surprisingly, this statistic has fueled civil rights groups, Congress, and the courts to ask if we as a nation are executing more blacks than whites merely because of the color of their skin. Are we administering the death penalty unfairly? Are we a nation of bigots set upon punishing an entire race of people merely because they are America's ignored minority?

This is one of many questions that the attorneys for William Henry Furman asked themselves following Furman's conviction and sentencing to death by a Chatham County, Georgia, Superior Court jury. It was one of the main questions they intended to present to the court if they received the retrial they requested following the conviction.

But Furman's request for a retrial was denied, so his attorneys took the next step in the lengthy and often complicated process of legal appeals. They petitioned the state's Supreme Court to review the case in the hopes that the court would overturn the death sentence handed down to Furman. The Supreme Court of Georgia responded by scheduling a review of the case *Furman* v. *Georgia* for April 24, 1969. Now the attorneys for William Henry Furman would begin their work in earnest. And they knew it would not hurt to pray a little, too.

A Case for Furman

CHAPTER 3

Clarence Mayfield, the attorney selected to write the brief, or written argument, of Furman's case for the Supreme Court of Georgia, knew he faced an uphill battle. As he researched material on capital punishment and the death penalty in America, he discovered that courts throughout history have considered execution to be a perfectly acceptable form of punishment. The only exception appeared to be when the manner of execution was either inhumane or barbarous—when it caused a person unnecessary pain or suffering. Certainly execution by electrocution—as Furman most likely faced—was neither inhumane or barbarous. At least, the United States Supreme Court had never found it to be so.

So Mayfield, a feisty courtroom advocate and a thorough researcher, set about the long and difficult job of locating legal precedents and reviewing previous court and historical documents that might prove beneficial to Furman's case. One of the United States Supreme Court cases he found most interesting was *Trop* v. *Dulles*, which addressed the question of Eighth Amendment rights.

In *Trop*, the petitioner, a native-born American citizen, was charged with and convicted of desertion from the military during time of war. He faced a sentence ranging from several years in prison to execution. He received a relatively light sentence, and eight years later, after serving his term in prison, applied for a passport in order to travel overseas. He was turned down on the grounds that he had lost his citizenship as a result of his wartime offense.

The United States Supreme Court, in reviewing the case, found that the punishment of being stripped of one's citizenship was "cruel and unusual," as prohibited by the Eighth Amendment. In his opinion, Chief Justice Earl Warren wrote, "The Amendment must draw its meaning from evolving standards of decency that mark the progress of a maturing society."

Warren went on to say that denationalization (being forced to give up one's citizenship) was a form of punishment more primitive and cruel than torture. Warren wrote: "It destroys for the individual the political existence that was centuries in the development. The punishment strips the citizen of his status in the national and international political community. . . . In short, the expatriate has lost the right to have rights."[1]

To Mayfield, Warren's opinion said that what may have been socially acceptable punishment ten, twenty, or thirty years ago may not be so today. As societies grow, as people become better educated and more concerned about the welfare of their fellow human beings, their attitudes toward crime and punishment change. In his historical research, Mayfield discovered several interesting facts about crime and punishment that supported Warren's opinion.

Prior to the Norman invasion of England in A.D. 1050, payments for an injury to another person were made directly to the victim or his relatives, according to the social rank of the injured party and the extent of the injury—a wounded arm, a broken leg, or even death warranted payment. The amount, instead of being fixed by the English Crown, was settled upon informally by impartial parties, "by the oath of honest men of the neighbourhood."[2]

By A.D. 1215, when the Magna Carta (or Magna Charta) was written, the informal custom of imposing fines for injuries against another person had disappeared. The Magna Carta, which was the first set of laws devoted to providing basic human rights for English citizens, reinstated this system. Now, for the first time, the process of imposing fines was formally set into law— along with some limitations. One translation of Article 20 of the Magna Carta reads, "A free man shall not be amerced [fined] for a slight offence, except in accordance with the degree of the offence; and for a grave offence he shall be amerced in accordance with the gravity of the offence."

By formalizing the fines and similar penalties, the English Crown was attempting "to eliminate the arbitrary element"[3] from such matters and to force English citizens to conform to the king's rules.

By the late 1600s, the process of imposing fines had changed once again. The English Bill of Rights, enacted on December 16, 1689, was concerned mostly with the discriminatory and irregular application of harsh penalties. Its aim was to ban all arbitrary and discriminatory penalties of a severe nature. The bill said:

> Following the Norman conquest of England in 1066, the old system of penalties, which ensured equality between crime and punishment, suddenly disappeared. By the time systematic judicial records were kept, its demise was almost complete. With the exception of certain grave crimes for which the punishment was death or outlawry, the arbitrary fine was replaced by a discretionary amercement [fine]. Although [the fine's] discretionary character allowed the circumstances of each case to be taken into account and the level of cash penalties to be decreased or increased accordingly, the [fine] presented an opportunity for excessive or oppressive [penalties].
>
> The problem of excessive [fines] became so prevalent that three chapters of the Magna Carta were devoted to their regulation.[4]

The English Bill of Rights stated that "excessive bail ought not to be required, nor excessive fines imposed, nor cruel and unusual punishments inflicted." These were the same words that America's Founding Fathers chose for the United States Constitution's Eighth Amendment, which passed into law in 1791—more than a century after the English Bill of Rights had come into existence an ocean away.

Similar provisions had been written into Virginia's Constitution in 1776, as well as into the constitutions of eight other states. The Northwest Ordinance, adopted by the United States Congress of Confederation in 1787 to create and govern the Northwest Territory, likewise included a prohibition of "cruel and unusual punishments."

But the question of what exactly made up "cruel and unusual punishments" had never been satisfactorily answered—either by the courts or by the legislatures. When the First Congress met to draft the first ten amendments to the United States Constitution, a representative from South Carolina objected to the words "cruel and unusual punishments" as being too indefinite and open to debate. Apparently, this was still the case.

So, as Mayfield met with his research staff to consider the best argument for his client's appeal to the Supreme Court of Georgia, he was faced with two major questions. First, was the death sentence that had been handed out to Furman cruel and unusual punishment? And second, what exactly was cruel and unusual punishment?

Mayfield knew that before he could convince the court that Furman's punishment was too harsh, he would have to persuade the court to settle on a definition of "cruel and unusual"—something no other court had been willing or able to do since the very birth of America's legal system.

Mayfield and his staff began diligently researching the question of cruel and unusual punishment. They searched old law volumes, reviewed English legal history, and scoured court precedents that might shed new light on the question. Certainly the notion of selective or irregular use of criminal penalties—including the death penalty—suggested that it was cruel and unusual to apply such penalties to members of minority groups whose numbers are few, who are outcasts of society, and who are unpopular with society, especially when that same society was unwilling to accept the same penalties handed out across the board.

It was one thing, apparently, to sentence a black man with a sixth-grade education to death for the accidental murder of a white man who was the father of five. It was quite another to sentence a white man for the same crime.

The attorney's review of legal history turned up another interesting case, *McGautha* v. *California*. Early in the afternoon of February 14, 1967, Dennis McGautha and an associate entered the business of Mrs. Pon Lock and robbed her at gunpoint of three hundred dollars. Three hours later, the same two bandits entered a store owned by Mrs. Benjamin Smetana. During the robbery, one of the bandits shot and killed her husband.

A mug shot of Dennis McGautha taken in 1970.

Although it was never proved, evidence pointed to McGautha as the murderer.

Both men were captured, tried, and convicted of two counts of armed robbery and one count of first-degree murder. The jurors, who had the task of assigning punishment as they saw fit, sentenced McGautha to death and his accomplice to life imprisonment.

In his appeal, McGautha claimed that the practice of allowing the jury to assign the death penalty without strict guidelines and standards for doing so violated his right to due process of law.

After the case had wound its way through the California courts, it finally was reviewed by the United States Supreme Court, which upheld the two sentences—despite a lack of rigid standards for the jury to use in determining who would die and who would live. The Court noted that from the beginning of America's legal system, there was a "rebellion against the common-law rule imposing a mandatory death sentence on all convicted murderers."[5]

The remedy to such sweeping impositions of the death penalty for all murders had seemed obvious—selective executions. But because selective executions placed a severe strain on juries, who were charged with the task of determining who would live and who would die, the juries soon began limiting the death penalty to those people who were found guilty of premeditated murder—murder that had been carefully planned and carried out.

But even here it became obvious that the system was not working properly. Juries often encountered difficulties in determining whether or not a murder had been premeditated. They eventually began taking the law into their own hands by refusing to convict criminals of murder, even when it was obvious that they had committed the crime. In this way, the jury members sidestepped the tricky question of premeditation and the personal consequences of sentencing someone to death.

In response, several state legislatures began putting aside the requirement of premeditation. They adopted a policy that in effect granted juries the discretion to decide on a case-by-case basis which murders would be punishable by death and which would not—regardless of premeditation. Juries (or, in some cases, judges) soon found themselves with the nearly unlimited power of allowing the accused to live or of sentencing him to die.

In upholding the sentence in *McGautha*, Justice John Harlan felt that giving a jury such unlimited discretion was constitutional. He could not see how doing otherwise was practical. It would not be possible, he wrote, "to identify before the fact those homicides for which the slayer should die"[6] and to impose a mandatory death sentence on the murderer. Only the jury, he reasoned, was in a position to impose such a sentence, and then only on a case-by-case basis.

Did this, Mayfield intended to ask the Supreme Court of Georgia, constitute cruel and unusual punishment? After all, it set some people apart from others and

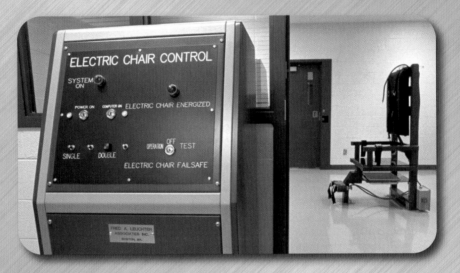

After the McGautha case, juries soon began limiting the death penalty to those people who were found guilty of premeditated murder. It was up to juries to decide who might be sent to an electric chair like this one.

created the opportunity for discrimination against people of certain races, religions, or social and economic classes.

Furman's attorney then reviewed a study of capital cases in Texas between the years of 1924 and 1968. The study showed that the death penalty had been applied unequally. Most of the accused during that period were poor, young, and uneducated. Seventy-five of the 460 cases involved codefendants who, under Texas law, were given separate trials. In several instances where a white and a black man were codefendants, the white man was often sentenced to life imprisonment or less, while the black man was given the death penalty.

The study showed that this held true for the crime of rape as well as for that of murder. A black man convicted of rape in the state of Texas was far more likely to get the death penalty than a term, or limited, sentence. A white or Latino man was far more likely to get a term sentence than the death penalty.

Warden Lewis E. Lawes of Sing Sing Prison confirmed what that and similar studies showed about racial inequalities:

> Not only does capital punishment fail in its justification, but no punishment could be invented with so many inherent defects. It is an unequal punishment in the way it is applied to the rich and to the poor. The defendant of wealth and position never goes to the electric chair or to the gallows. Juries do not intentionally favour the rich; the law is theoretically impartial, but the defendant with ample means is able to have his case presented with every favorable aspect, while the poor defendant [such as Furman] often has

a lawyer assigned by the court. Sometimes such assignment is considered part of political patronage; usually the lawyer assigned has had no experience whatever in a capital case.[7]

Violations of human rights and discrimination in the law were nothing new, of course. Wherever judges and juries sat in judgment of the accused, abuses occurred. Discretion in applying the death penalty enabled the penalty to be applied selectively. This opened up the opportunity for prejudice against the accused, particularly if he was poor, hated, lacking political power, or was a member of an unpopular minority.

In ancient India, with its many castes, or social classes, Hindu law exempted a Brahman, who was at the top of the caste system, from capital punishment. Everyone else was subject to execution. In effect, punishment increased in severity as social status declined.

Mayfield feared that the same system of prejudicial punishment had somehow evolved in America. Slowly, quietly, and unintentionally—but it had evolved. Furman was only the latest in a long string of the underprivileged to bear the brunt of discrimination within America's legal system. Now Mayfield had to convince Georgia's highest court that such discrimination had no place within the halls of American justice.

As the day the Supreme Court of Georgia had set aside to review Furman's case drew near, Mayfield decided to request an overturn of the death penalty imposed upon Furman by the lower court. For justification he planned to use both theoretical principles and legal technicalities.

He would first ask that the court overturn Furman's conviction because one prospective juror in the original superior court trial had been dismissed because of his opposition to the death penalty. Mayfield knew he had little hope that the Supreme Court of Georgia would consider this grounds for overturning the lower court's findings, but it was nonetheless worth a try.

Next, Mayfield would argue that Furman had not been advised of his constitutional rights at the time of his arrest, and therefore, his statements regarding the crime had been improperly admitted during the original trial. Naturally, Mayfield expected the state to argue that Furman had been read his rights, so this argument, too, was probably a long shot.

He would also argue that since Furman had been held in jail for more than the forty-eight-hour legal maximum before being charged, the jury's verdict should be overturned. There was a possibility here that the Supreme Court of Georgia would be moved by the state's obvious error in holding Furman longer than it should have, but once again it was far from a sure thing.

He would argue, too, that the four days that passed before the hearing was held to determine whether or not Furman was mentally competent to stand trial was a basis for overturning the jury's verdict—another long shot, but worth trying.

Finally, Mayfield planned to argue that the Georgia state laws authorizing capital punishment violated the

United States Constitution's prohibitions against cruel and unusual punishment. While this was the best argument for overturning the lower court's ruling, the fact that it had never before been used successfully in a court of law did not bode well for Furman.

Yet despite the limited chance for success, Mayfield knew that he had to press on with the case. He could do no more than his best, and he was convinced that Furman did not deserve to be put to death. Now it was merely a matter of writing a brief—a lawyer's written argument—that would convince the justices of the Supreme Court of Georgia that he was right.

A Case for the State of Georgia

CHAPTER 4

The state received notification that the defense attorneys in *Furman* v. *Georgia* had successfully filed a motion for review by the Supreme Court of Georgia. The state's attorneys— headed by District Attorney Andrew J. Ryan and backed up by Attorney General Marion O. Gordon, Assistant Attorney General Larry H. Evans, and attorney Robert E. Baker— began preparing their brief for the defense of the death penalty handed out to William Henry Furman.

Not knowing exactly what arguments Furman's attorneys would advance on his behalf, the state's attorneys instructed their staff to prepare as wide a defense as possible. This would include everything from the constitutionality of executions in general to the question of discrimination against blacks within the penal system in Georgia.

The state's attorneys found several United States Supreme Court decisions in support of executions for capital crimes. In *Wilkerson* v. *Utah* (1878), a unanimous opinion held executions to be constitutional. It then specifically upheld the constitutionality of execution by firing squad, saying: "Cruel and unusual punishments are forbidden by the Constitution, but the authorities . . . are quite sufficient to show that the punishment of shooting as a mode of executing the death penalty for the crime of murder in the first degree is not included in that category [of cruel and unusual punishments]."[1]

Eleven years later, the Court reviewed a case in which it tried to determine how cruelty and unusualness related to one another. In *In* re *Kemmler* (1890), the petitioner, a convicted murderer, was sentenced to die in the electric chair—one of the earliest uses of electrocution on record. Among other claims, Kemmler insisted that electrocution violated the "cruel and unusual" punishment clause of the Eighth Amendment. The Court did not agree, ruling that despite the fact that electrocution might be considered unusual, it was hardly cruel. In fact, it was apparently extremely humane, since death by electrocution came quickly and painlessly. In its decision, the Court said: "Punishments are cruel when they involve torture or a lingering death; but the punishment of death is not cruel, within the meaning of that word as used in the Constitution. It implies there

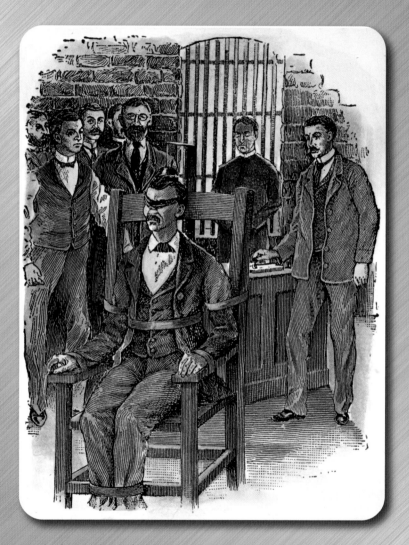

This drawing depicts the execution of William Kemmler on August 6, 1890.
He was the first person ever to die in the electric chair.

is something inhuman and barbarous, something more than the mere extinguishment of life."[2]

The Georgia state attorneys found numerous other references and precedents. On nearly every occasion that the question of the constitutionality of the death penalty had been presented to the United States Supreme Court, the justices resolved the issue in favor of execution. Nowhere in the Constitution, apparently, was the death penalty expressly forbidden.

With these questions out of the way, the state's attorneys next tackled the question of discrimination. Did Georgia's court system discriminate against blacks? And if so, did that mean that it had discriminated against Furman?

In their research, the attorneys discovered penal system records that seemed to refute the discrimination argument. The greater percentage of blacks than whites executed by Georgia prisons, according to the statistics, was due to a greater percentage of blacks making up the overall prison population in Georgia. That would seem to support the state's contention that it did not discriminate against blacks.

Furthermore, the attorneys would argue, the Georgia penal system statistics taken from the period from 1930 to 1968, because of their very age, failed to take into account the changes in Georgia's criminal justice system that had recently taken place. More current statistics showed that capital criminals were receiving greater due process of the law than at any other time in history. Therefore, Furman—like those convicted

Georgia State Prison in 2007. The state's case in *Furman* v. *Georgia* rested on their assertion that the greater percentage of blacks than whites facing the death penalty in Georgia was a fair reflection of the number of blacks and whites in Georgia's prison population.

criminals sentenced to death just before him—had received the benefits of Georgia's increased concern for individual rights, regardless of race.

The state's attorneys found several United States Supreme Court decisions affirming the jury's right to set sentencing in murder cases. In *Williams* v. *New York* (1949), Justice Murphy defended this right by saying that the jury acts as a representative of the community. Its decisions are therefore those of the society against which the crime was committed. Its verdicts are a reflection of the feelings of the community.

Furthermore, the attorneys found statistics that showed that the majority of Americans were *not* opposed to the death penalty when imposed by a judge or a jury after a fair trial ensuring due process of law. And certainly the United States Constitution guarantees due process. Nowhere in the Constitution was there a restriction preventing individual states from imposing and carrying out sentencing. This was a point the state's attorneys were particularly anxious to bring out.

While guaranteeing each United States citizen equal rights, the Fourteenth Amendment does prohibit some actions by the states: "No State shall make or enforce any law which shall abridge the privileges or immunities of citizens of the United States; nor shall any State deprive any person of life, liberty or property, without due process of law; nor deny to any person within its jurisdiction the equal protection of the laws."

But, the attorneys would argue, by prohibiting a state from depriving a person of life *without due process of law*, the amendment therefore granted a state the right to take a person's life *with due process of law*.

Certainly, the state's attorneys were prepared to argue, the state had provided Furman with due process of law by trying him in a Georgia criminal courtroom in a trial heard by his peers—fellow citizens of the state of Georgia. Having done so, it was then reasonable to assume that the state had met all of its requirements under the Fourteenth Amendment. Therefore, Georgia had every right to sentence Furman to death.

Convinced that the state of Georgia had done its job in preparing its defense of the death penalty against Furman—and knowing that no court had ever over-turned a death sentence based upon the Eighth or Fourteenth Amendments—the state's attorneys sub-mitted their brief and awaited the Supreme Court of Georgia review with confidence.

The attorneys' confidence, it would soon turn out, was well placed.

On April 24, 1969, the Supreme Court of Georgia met to deliver its decision. After a short review of the case, Chief Justice Duckworth presented a brief opening summary followed by the official opinion of the court: "This case involves the crime of murder by shooting, occurring during a burglary after the intruder had been discovered by the deceased, who was then shot through a closed door. The accused was indicted, tried, and con-victed. . . . A motion for new trial . . . was filed, heard, and overruled, and the appeal is from the judgment, after conviction, and sentence."[3]

The opinion that followed dealt first with Mayfield's contention that the dismissal of a juror who was opposed to capital punishment was grounds for overturning Furman's conviction and the granting of a new trial: "A juror having been excluded for cause because he stated that his opposition to the death penalty would affect his decision as to a defendant's guilt, his exclusion did not fall within the rule . . . and the court did not err in excusing him for cause. There is no merit in the amended motion complaining that the exclusion violated the rule."[4]

Next, the opinion addressed the question of whether or not Furman's rights had been violated at the time of his arrest. In reviewing the facts surrounding Furman's arrest, the court found that upon his arrest, the accused had his constitutional rights explained to him—including the right to remain silent, the right of counsel, and that anything he said might be used against him in court—and that he thereafter freely, voluntarily, and knowingly made certain statements in regard to the crime, the same was admissible both legally and factually, and all the requirements of 1966's *Miranda* v. *Arizona* "have been complied with fully and completely. We find no merit in the contention of counsel that his [Furman's] constitutional rights have been violated."[5]

Since the court found that Furman's rights had not been violated at the time of his arrest, it also found that all of the evidence submitted during the superior court trial, including the murder weapon with Furman's fingerprints on it, had been legally admitted to court.

The court also found that despite the fact that Furman was not granted a hearing on his mental condition within forty-eight hours, as required by Georgia state law, the state was within its rights to try, convict, and sentence the defendant:

> The record discloses that the accused was arrested on August 11, 1967, and a commitment hearing held on August 15, 1967. While [the Georgia State] Code . . . requires a hearing within 48 hours, nevertheless, a detention or imprisonment beyond a reasonable time does not render the verdict of a jury after indictment illegal or void. It has already been held above that the evidence of fingerprints, pistol, and admissions which were obtained after his arrest could be used against him, and no secret inquisition or interrogation [that might be grounds for overturning Furman's conviction] is claimed in this case.[6]

Perhaps most important of all, the court in its opinion ruled that the state had not violated the Constitution's "cruel and unusual punishment" clause by sentencing Furman to death.

"The statutes of this State authorizing capital punishment have repeatedly been held not to be cruel and unusual punishment in violation of the Constitution. . . . Hence, there is no merit in this complaint."[7]

In its conclusion, the court summed up its reasons for upholding Furman's conviction and sentencing:

> The admission in open court by the accused in his unsworn statement that, during the period in which he was involved in the commission of a criminal act at the home of the deceased, he accidentally tripped over

a wire in leaving the premises, causing the gun to go off, together with other facts and circumstances surrounding the death of the deceased by violent means, was sufficient to support the verdict of guilty of murder, and the general grounds of the motion for new trial are not meritorious. . . .

Having considered every enumeration of error argued by [Furman's] counsel in his brief and finding no reversible error, the judgment is Affirmed.

All the Justices concur.[8]

To the Highest Court

CHAPTER
5

Within two years of Furman's arrest, trial, and conviction for murder, the Supreme Court of Georgia had reviewed the case on appeal. It ruled unanimously in favor of upholding the lower court's decision.

Throughout the proceedings, William Henry Furman had been imprisoned pending review by the state's highest court. He now awaited the date of his execution. At least that was what the state's attorneys assumed.

But Furman's attorneys had other ideas. While they had been busy preparing their case for the Supreme Court of Georgia, Anthony G. Amsterdam, a respected trial lawyer and a professor at California's Stanford Law School, had been enlisted by the National Association for the Advancement of Colored People (NAACP) to research the legal precedents and construct arguments that might convince a higher court to overturn Furman's death sentence. Amsterdam, a longtime consultant for the NAACP, went to work with that group's Legal Defense Fund (LDF) to have the death penalty overturned on the grounds of unconstitutionality. The LDF hoped to use the momentum it had gained in 1954 in the Supreme Court's invalidation of segregation in *Brown* v. *Board of Education* to pressure the Court to ban capital punishment.

So, shortly after the Supreme Court of Georgia issued its ruling, Furman's attorneys filed a petition for certiorari—a request to move the case to the United States Supreme Court. Within days, the Supreme Court agreed to hear the case. Now, it was up to America's judicial system to decide the fate of William Henry Furman—and, even more importantly, the fate of the death penalty in America.

Both of the principal attorneys in the Furman case—Amsterdam and Dorothy T. Beasley, the assistant attorney general who had been chosen to argue the case for the state of Georgia—were anxious to begin their oral arguments before the Supreme Court.

Amsterdam hoped to prove not that Furman was innocent, for his guilt in committing the crimes of robbery and murder had been well established, but that the death penalty given to Furman was cruel and unusual punishment and therefore unconstitutional. He knew that a similar argument had failed to win over the

Supreme Court of Georgia. But he also knew that if he could prove the unconstitutionality of the death penalty to the United States Supreme Court, Furman's sentence would be overturned in favor of life imprisonment—most likely with the chance for parole.

Beasley, on the other hand, would argue that the Georgia death penalty was constitutional, that the case of *Furman* had met all of the requirements of the United States Constitution's Eighth and Fourteenth Amendments, and that the sentence handed out to William Henry Furman should therefore be allowed to stand.

At 11:09 A.M. on Monday, January 17, 1972, the two attorneys met inside the hallowed halls of the Supreme Court building in Washington, D.C., where they would soon begin their arguments before the highest court in the land.

Because there were three death penalty cases being considered by the Court that day (*Furman* v. *Georgia*, *Jackson* v. *Georgia*, and *Branch* v. *Texas*, the last two involving capital punishment verdicts for convicted rapists), the Court decided to combine the three cases into one.

The attorneys for Furman had originally petitioned that the Supreme Court grant a hearing, so Furman was the petitioner in the case and Amsterdam was the first attorney to present his argument. Following Amsterdam, Beasley, acting on behalf of the state of Georgia, would present the case for the respondent.

Anthony Amsterdam rose from his seat and began his opening arguments with a brief discussion of society's view concerning the death penalty: "We are talking about a progressive trend which has brought virtually every nation in the Western Hemisphere, with the possible exception of Paraguay and Chile, to abolish the death penalty. We are talking about a progressive trend which has caused all of the English-speaking nations of the world, except some of the American states and four states in Australia, to abolish the death penalty."[1]

One of the justices then asked Amsterdam if he thought it possible that the death penalty might be unconstitutional except in a few specific cases—such as when a prison inmate kills another inmate or a prison guard. Amsterdam replied that it might be possible, but he pointed out that placing such restrictions on the death penalty would require that new laws be passed by Congress and that they then be tested by the Court.

Then Amsterdam went on to discuss how unevenly the death penalty was handed out in American courts: "To start with . . . juries only do return about a hundred death verdicts a year. Now, to understand how small that is, you have to compare it with the number of crimes punishable by death. It's a very difficult thing to do. . . . What you find out is that juries don't apply the death penalty in perhaps more than one out of twelve or thirteen, at the very most, cases in which they could. And maybe a half or a third of those people are actually executed."[2]

When the justices asked Amsterdam if he had any knowledge of what types of prisoners the state of

Georgia executes, the attorney found himself squarely facing the very crux of his argument—that death sentences in Georgia are handed out indiscriminately, at the whim of a judge or jury, and not based upon objective rules.

"There is nothing in the record," said Amsterdam, "but the figures are perfectly plain—the National Prisoners Statistics. Georgia executes black people."[3]

Amsterdam went on to argue that when a nation the size of America executes so few people in the course of a year, the reason is absolutely clear. Capital punishment is regarded by most Americans as indecent and uncivilized, he said, despite the fact that forty-three states still allowed the death penalty at that time.

Then Amsterdam argued that the reason the death penalty had not been abolished throughout the United States before 1972 was that since so few executions took place, there was no pressing need to repeal the laws allowing the executions. "The very fact that capital punishment comes to be as rarely and as infrequently and as [subjectively] imposed as it is takes the pressure off the legislature, quite simply, to do anything about it."[4]

Then the Court asked Amsterdam how many people were awaiting execution in California when the California legislature most recently considered abolishing the death penalty. The attorney replied that there were approximately eighty-five or ninety. The Court asked how Amsterdam could consider that many prisoners awaiting execution in California alone to be a "small" number. Amsterdam replied:

What you're talking about is an accumulation on death row over a period of time of twelve or thirteen years. You're talking about eighty people in a prison system that houses thousands and thousands and thousands of people. You are talking about—and I think this is relevant—you are talking about eighty people of whom at that time twenty-five or thirty . . . were members of minority groups . . . California counts Chicanos as white for these purposes, something which, for one who lives in California, I find rather strange in terms of the question of who bears the brunt of the penalties.[5]

As Amsterdam concluded his oral arguments, stating that he wanted to reserve some time for a rebuttal to Georgia's assistant attorney general, one of the justices asked Amsterdam if he, the justice, had understood all of the attorney's points clearly:

Even assuming that retribution is a permissible ingredient of punishment, even assuming that rational people could conclude that the death sentence is the maximum deterrent with the minimum [of] unnecessary cruelty—death in the electric chair—even assuming we're dealing with somebody who is not capable of being rehabilitated, an incorrigible person, even assuming that rational people can conclude that this punishment under these circumstances is the most efficient and the most inexpensive and the most—and that ensures the most complete isolation of the convicted man from ever getting back into society—even assuming all of those things, which are the basic arguments made by your brothers and sisters on the other side [of the death penalty question], you say it is still [unconstitutional under] the Eighth Amendment? Am I right in my understanding of that?[6]

Amsterdam agreed, adding that "it is our submission that [in] accepting each and every one of those propositions, the death penalty is a cruel and unusual punishment."[7]

So, after arguing *Furman* for nearly half an hour, Amsterdam's case came down to a few specific points that could be summed up neatly.

Following Amsterdam's arguments, Chief Justice Warren Burger turned to Dorothy Beasley, who was preparing to argue the case for Georgia.

Beasley opened her arguments by saying that in questioning whether or not death was cruel and unusual punishment as prohibited by the Eighth Amendment, the petitioners had overlooked one important point— due process of law, as guaranteed by the Fourteenth Amendment. Beasley continued: "What the Fourteenth Amendment provides is that . . . no state may deprive any person of life, liberty, or property without due process of law. Now that was written in 1868, long after the Fifth—the Eighth and the Fifth Amendments were written. So that when the restriction was made on the State by way of the Fourteenth Amendment, the death penalty was already recognized and the restriction on the states was only that they not deprive a man of his life or liberty or property without due process of law."[8]

Trying to determine if Beasley was saying that the Fourteenth Amendment made acceptable any form of

Anthony G. Amsterdam (center), a respected trial lawyer and a professor of law at California's Stanford University Law School, was enlisted to research the legal precedents and construct arguments that might convince a higher court to overturn Furman's death sentence.

punishment that the state wanted to inflict, the Court asked if she thought the state could boil a prisoner in oil.

"I think not, Your Honor," she replied, "because the terms of due process of law and the taking of life or property does not include corporal punishment of that type. . . . What we had at the beginning of our country was the understanding that it may not impose torture, and that [boiling in oil] of course would be torture, as would horsewhipping, as Mr. Justice Stewart mentions. Those things were taken out of the realm of punishment at the very beginning [of America's legal system] with . . . the Bill of Rights."[9]

When asked what standard Beasley would use to determine which punishments were acceptable and which were cruel and unusual, she replied:

> It is the same standard that has been used by this Court in so many cases in applying the due process clause: Is it a matter of fundamental fairness? Is it a concept of or ordered liberties. . . . That's where . . . cruel and unusual punishment comes into the concept of ordered liberty—of fundamental fairness. And I think that so long as the State utilizes fundamental fairness in dealing with its penal system and imposing penalties, that those penalties may be used, particularly since the states were specifically permitted by the Fourteenth Amendment to utilize the taking of life, so long as it was done with due process of law. And I think that's one of the basic fallacies in most of the arguments that are made by petitioners [Furman and his attorneys], because [they talk] about rarity and discrimination. Well, obviously, then, it is not with

due process of law if it's arbitrary, and that is the limitation on the states.[10]

At that point, the Court brought up a series of questions that seemed to cast a shadow over Beasley's argument.

THE COURT: Mrs. Beasley, didn't the *Francis* case take into cognizance that the State could not impose unnecessary pain—the *Francis* case of this Court?

MRS. BEASLEY: Yes, sir. I am aware of that case.

THE COURT: They recognized a little more than just due process, didn't they?

MRS. BEASLEY: But that was—

THE COURT: Didn't this Court in that case recognize that the Eighth Amendment was applicable to the states?

MRS. BEASLEY: Yes, insofar—

THE COURT: And you're now saying it's not?

After reassuring the Court that she was not denying the importance of the states' upholding the principles of the Eighth Amendment, Beasley went on to argue that the death penalty in itself should not be considered cruel and unusual punishment. The Fourteenth Amendment, she insisted, specifically reserved the states' rights to impose the death penalty.

In *Louisiana ex rel. Francis* v. *Reswebe* (1947), the petitioner had been convicted and sentenced to death. He was placed in the state's electric chair and subjected to an electrical current. Through some mechanical failure, the current was too low to cause his death. Francis was taken from the execution chamber and returned to prison. Meanwhile, a new execution date was set. Francis objected, claiming that subjecting him a second time to the electric chair was cruel and unusual punishment. The Supreme Court disagreed, saying that "[t]he fact that an unforeseeable accident prevented the prompt consummation [carrying out] of the sentence cannot . . . add an element of cruelty to a subsequent execution."[11]

At that point, the Court asked if the "cruel and unusual punishment" clause in the Eighth Amendment was meant to be applied without discrimination.

"Oh, yes, indeed," said Beasley. "It should be applied in a nondiscriminatory manner."[12]

Then Justice William O. Douglas asked if Beasley had any statistics relating to what kinds of people the state of Georgia executed.

Beasley replied:

Mr. Justice Douglas, we submitted in our brief a chart that I obviously have made up from the statistics that we were able to gather from the [Georgia] Department of Corrections showing those people now under death penalty in Georgia. And I don't think that you could say that there's any one class, or that that class has been discriminated against. Moreover, even if there was shown to be discrimination—and we submit that there was not shown to be discrimination—that that would not invalidate the death penalty *per se* but it would be a violation of the equal protection clause, not the Eighth Amendment. In other words, you may have discrimination in the sentencing in larceny [theft], that only black people get the maximum for larceny. Well, obviously, that would be discriminatory. But that wouldn't mean that you couldn't sentence anybody for twenty years imprisonment for larceny. It would simply mean that, in those cases where there was discrimination, those sentences were invalid.[13]

Then the Court asked if the question of discrimination in applying the death penalty had ever been considered by a Georgia court.

"I think not," Beasley replied, "because I don't think that it's had the opportunity to do so . . . . In *Furman* the argument wasn't even made in the lower court. It simply was stated, but no argument was made. And there was a very, very short argument, as was pointed out in our brief, in the brief to the Supreme Court of Georgia, citing merely the bald statistics of how many white people and how many black people had been executed since 1930, up to 1968. Well, that doesn't prove that the death penalty is cruel and unusual punishment."[14]

Then, arguing against Amsterdam's contention that most Americans consider the death penalty to be indecent and uncivilized, Beasley said, "In the two cases which Georgia has standing before the [Supreme] Court—as a matter of fact, in *Furman* right now before the Court—there was only one person out of the total panel of 48 [potential jurors] . . . who said that they were so against the death penalty that they could never impose it in any case."[15]

Finally, in her closing arguments, Beasley cited several United States Supreme Court cases that held that the legislature had the right to pass whatever laws it wanted to pass, and that it was the Court's right to determine if those laws were constitutional. But the Fourteenth Amendment, she insisted, gave the states the specific right to administer the death penalty—and to decide to whom it did so—so long as the accused was granted due process of law.

Following Beasley's arguments, Anthony Amsterdam received three minutes for rebuttal, and he used the time well. He pointed out first that a small number of jurors in only two cases did not represent the attitude of an entire nation toward capital punishment.

Then Amsterdam asked the Court why it should step in to determine the question of whether or not capital punishment was constitutional. Why not simply let the death penalty issue slowly fade away, as it seemed to be doing anyway? He said:

> The answer is [in] the case [of] *Furman* v. *Georgia* where what you have is a regular garden-variety burglary/murder, an unintended killing. Somebody shot through the door. The case is submitted on the theory that it was an unintended killing. There are thousands of these. The jury comes back with death. The defendant is black; the victim is white. . . .
>
> There are Georgia figures in this record . . . thirty-three people on death row, twenty-seven of them black, six white. The reason why juries can't be permitted to go on doing what they've done and slowly, [inevitably] do away with the death penalty

The original ten amendments to the United States Constitution were known as the Bill of Rights. Furman's lawyers argued that imposing a death sentence on him would violate the Eighth Amendment, which forbids cruel and unusual punishment. Dorothy T. Beasley, the assistant attorney general of Georgia, argued that the Georgia death penalty was constitutional and met the requirements of the Constitution's Eighth and Fourteenth Amendments.

themselves is that in individual and particular cases, there are going to be [mistakes], depending largely on the color of the defendant's skin and the ugliness of his person.[16]

With that, Amsterdam concluded his case. It seemed to have gone well. At least the justices had not appeared to have been as doubtful of his arguments as they had been of Beasley's. Yet, in his many years of work as a trial lawyer and a professor at Stanford Law School, Anthony Amsterdam had learned the hard way that you simply could not take anything for granted. In court, as in a game of chess, you never knew who would emerge the victor until the game was over.

The justices, Amsterdam realized, could reach a number of different conclusions. They could decide that Furman was correct and the death sentence he received was cruel and unusual punishment. They could rule that the state of Georgia was right and that the death penalty was protected by the Fourteenth Amendment. They could even decide against issuing any ruling at all—either sending the case back to the lower courts for further consideration or requesting a reargument before the Supreme Court.

There would be a time to celebrate, Amsterdam knew—or there would be a time to mourn. But no one could yet tell when either time would come. Not even the justices themselves.

The Decision

CHAPTER 6

Furman's attorney, Anthony Amsterdam, and Georgia's assistant attorney general, Dorothy Beasley, each received a telephone call from the clerk of the Court on June 28, 1972— more than five months after they had argued the case of *Furman* v. *Georgia* before a packed courtroom. The justices had reached a decision, they were told. They planned to announce it the next day.

That was all there was to it. No fanfare. No celebration. Just a simple statement of fact.

The call left Amsterdam wondering just how the Court had decided to vote. Sometimes, when an attorney finishes his oral arguments, he feels good about himself, good about the job he has done before the

Court, and confident about the results (as confident as one can ever be, at any rate).

And then the waiting begins. Each day that goes by seems like an eternity. And by the time the eternities have passed, the attorney has ended up wondering just how good a job he did after all—and wondering if he could have done better.

So when the nine justices entered the Supreme Court building on the morning of June 29, nobody knew for sure how they had voted. But a gallery packed with journalists, law students, and curious citizens was ready to wait for as long as it took for the Court to read its decision.

It did not take long. After settling down to the business at hand, Chief Justice Warren Burger read the opinion of the Court in *Furman* v. *Georgia, Jackson* v. *Georgia*, and *Branch* v. *Texas*: "Petitioner in No. 69-5003 [Furman] was convicted of murder in Georgia and was sentenced to death pursuant to Georgia Code. . . . Certiorari was granted limited to the following question: Does the imposition and carrying out of the death penalty . . . constitute cruel and unusual punishment in violation of the Eighth and Fourteenth Amendments? The Court holds that the imposition and carrying out of the death penalty in these cases constitutes cruel and unusual punishment in violation of the Eighth and Fourteenth Amendments. The judgment in each case is therefore reversed."

The decision was a split vote, 5 to 4, with justices William O. Douglas, William J. Brennan, Jr., Potter

Stewart, Byron R. White, and Thurgood Marshall concurring, and justices Warren E. Burger, Harry A. Blackmun, Lewis F. Powell, Jr., and William H. Rehnquist dissenting. All nine justices filed separate opinions in support of their votes because all nine had different views on why the death penalty was—or was not—unconstitutional. The nine separate opinions tied a Supreme Court record.

In voting with the majority, Douglas said that he found it to be cruel and unusual punishment to apply the death penalty selectively to minorities whose numbers are few, who are outcasts of society, and who are unpopular, but whom society is willing to see suffer, although it would not tolerate the death penalty applied objectively in every case across the board—most notably, for white defendants convicted of the same crime. Douglas explained:

> The high service rendered by the 'cruel and unusual' punishment clause of the Eighth Amendment is to require legislatures to write penal laws that are evenhanded, nonselective, and nonarbitrary, and to require judges to see to it that general laws are not applied sparsely, selectively, and spottily to unpopular groups.
>
> A law that stated that anyone making more than $50,000 would be exempt from the death penalty would plainly fall, as would a law that in terms said that blacks, those who never went beyond the fifth grade in school, those who made less than $3,000 a year, or those who were unpopular or unstable should be the only people executed. A law which in

the overall view reaches that result in practice has no more sanctity than a law which in terms provides the same.

Thus, these discretionary statutes are unconstitutional [408 U.S. 238, 257] in their operation.[1]

Justice Brennan, agreeing with Douglas, said that the Eighth Amendment's prohibition against cruel and unusual punishment was not limited to torturous punishments or to punishments that were considered cruel and unusual at the time the Eighth Amendment was adopted. A punishment was cruel and unusual, he said, if it was not applied with human dignity and that since it was a denial of human dignity for a state arbitrarily to subject a person to an unusually severe punishment which society indicated that it did not regard as acceptable for the entire population, and which could not be shown to serve any penal purpose more effectively than a less drastic form of punishment, death was therefore cruel and unusual. Brennan said:

> Today death is a uniquely and unusually severe punishment. When examined by the principles applicable under the Cruel and Unusual Punishment Clause, death stands condemned as fatally offensive to human dignity. The punishment of death is therefore "cruel and unusual," and the States may no longer inflict it as a punishment for crimes. Rather than kill an arbitrary handful of criminals each year, the States will confine them in prison. "The State thereby suffers nothing and loses no power. The purpose of punishment is fulfilled, crime is repressed by penalties of just, not tormenting, severity, its repetition is

The Burger Court at the time of *Furman* v. *Georgia* (1972): (from left, front row) Potter Stewart, William O. Douglas, Warren E. Burger, William J. Brennan, Jr., and Byron R. White. From left, back row: Lewis F. Powell, Jr., Thurgood Marshall, Harry A. Blackmun, and William H. Rehnquist.

prevented, and hope is given for the reformation of the criminal."

I concur in the judgments of the Court.[2]

Stewart, in writing the shortest of the concurring opinions, said that the petitioners were among a capriciously selected random handful upon whom the sentence of death was imposed and that the Eighth and Fourteenth Amendments could not tolerate the infliction of a sentence of death under legal systems which permitted this unique penalty to be so wantonly and so freakishly imposed, but that it was unnecessary to reach the ultimate question of whether or not the infliction of the death penalty was constitutionally impermissible in all circumstances under the Eighth and Fourteenth Amendments. While he was opposed to the way the states were administering the death penalty, he was not ready to say that the death penalty could not be administered under different, and fairer, circumstances.

"These death sentences are cruel and unusual in the same way that being struck by lightning is cruel and unusual. For, of all the people convicted of rapes and murders in 1967 and 1968, many just as reprehensible as these, the petitioners are among a capriciously selected random handful upon whom the sentence of death has in fact been imposed. . . . For these reasons, I concur in the judgments of the Court."[3]

White, agreeing with Stewart, stated that as the state statutes involved in the case were administered, the death penalty was so infrequently imposed that the threat of execution was too rare to be of very much use to the criminal justice system. He added that it was unnecessary to decide whether or not the death penalty was unconstitutional. "In my judgment, what was done in these cases violated the Eighth Amendment."[4]

Marshall, in a long and rambling opinion bursting with references to legal precedents, agreed with the concurring justices. The death penalty, he said, violated the Eighth Amendment because it was an excessive and unnecessary punishment and because it was morally unacceptable to the majority of the people of the United States. He made it clear that in so deciding, he was not condemning the United States system of government, simply responding to its changing needs.

"Only in a free society could right triumph in difficult times, and could civilization record its magnificent advancement. In recognizing the humanity of our fellow beings, we pay ourselves the highest tribute. We achieve 'a major milestone in the long road up from barbarism' and join the approximately 70 other jurisdictions in the world which celebrate their regard for civilization and humanity by shunning capital punishment. I concur in the judgments of the Court."[5]

On the other hand, Chief Justice Burger disagreed bitterly with the majority, saying in his dissenting opinion that the constitutional prohibition against cruel and unusual punishments could not be interpreted as barring the death sentence from being used. And the Eighth Amendment did not prohibit all punishments that the states were unable to prove necessary to deter or control crime, he insisted. The Eighth Amendment was not concerned with the process by which a state determined that a particular punishment was to be imposed in any particular case.

The Eighth Amendment, he added, did not address the power of the legislature to grant juries the ability to decide what sentences to apply. To set aside the petitioners' death sentences in the present case on the grounds that prevailing sentencing practices did not meet Eighth Amendment standards was wrong.

Blackmun, also dissenting, agreed with Burger that the Eighth Amendment protections did not apply in this case. He added that his personal distaste for the death penalty was supported by the belief that capital punishment served no useful purpose that could be shown. He felt, too, that although the arguments against capital punishment might be a proper basis for the legislature to abolish the death penalty in the future, the courts should not take over the authorization of such abolishment under the disguise of an Eighth Amendment issue.

Powell, the third dissenting justice, stated that none of the opinions supporting the Court's decision provided a constitutional basis for the decision and that the case against the constitutionality of the death penalty fell far short, especially when viewed in light of the references to capital punishment in the Constitution, in previous Supreme Court cases, and in light of the duties of the state and federal legislatures to make the laws.

Rehnquist, in agreeing with his fellow dissenters, emphasized the need for judicial self-restraint and added that the broadest interpretation of the leading constitutional cases did not suggest that the Supreme Court granted the authority, either by the Founding Fathers or by the framers of the Fourteenth Amendment, to strike down laws that were based upon notions of policy or morality—even if a majority of the Supreme Court justices suddenly found them to be unacceptable to the nation.

So in its wildly split opinion, the Supreme Court reached two major decisions.

1. The imposition and carrying out of the death penalty constitutes cruel and unusual punishment, in violation of the Eighth and Fourteenth Amendments, at least where a person convicted in a state court for murder or rape is African American and is sentenced to death after a trial by a jury, which, under state law, has discretion to determine whether or not to impose the death penalty.[6]

2. Upon holding that the imposition and carrying out of the death penalty in certain cases constitutes cruel and unusual punishment, the United States Supreme Court will reverse state appellate court judgments . . . and the Supreme Court will call back the cases for further proceedings.[7]

This last decision was particularly important because it served notice on all the states that currently had prisoners awaiting execution. They would now be required to review each of the prisoner's cases and impose an alternate sentence, something short of execution—most probably, life imprisonment.

In the end, the Court had reached a monumental decision, one that would affect the sentencing in capital crimes in the United States for years to come. But as Justice Stewart had predicted, that did not mean that the state legislatures would never again be able to hand out the death sentence. And, indeed, within the span of a decade, they began doing just that.

Yesterday, Today, and Tomorrow

CHAPTER

7

Within the first few days following the *Furman* decision, legislators from some thirty-five states began scurrying to amend their statutes in regard to the death penalty. A number of states also began reviewing their laws against discrimination. After all, all three appellants in the *Furman* case had been black, a fact that awakened many civil rights organizations to the very real possibility that America's judicial system was biased. These groups would be sure to be watching the various state legislatures to see how they might react to the comments of the justices in regard to discriminatory sentencing based solely on race.

Furman had been overturned and the majority opinion of the Court had dealt a crippling blow to discrimination in the nation's judicial system. Yet, some civil rights groups were unhappy with the opinions of the dissenting justices, who seemed to ignore the question of racism in America's prisons. Because Chief Justice Burger and Justices Blackmun, Powell, and Rehnquist did not take a stand with the majority, some viewed them as being—if not in favor of a racially split system of justice—tacitly supportive of it.

While celebrations over *Furman* broke out around the nation, picket lines went up in several major cities, where civil rights groups demanded an accounting from the dissenting justices. Other protests came from groups who had been in favor of retaining the death penalty. Outspoken legislators, community leaders, and others demanded immediate changes in state laws that would bring the death penalty back—at least for specific offenses, such as the murder of policemen, prison offi-cials, and other law enforcement officers.

In California, a November 1972 referendum showed that most voters favored restoring the death penalty under certain circumstances. The California legisla-ture—and others around the country—began the long and difficult task of reviewing their laws regarding capital punishment. At the same time, efforts were begun to find ways of making the imprisonment of capital offenders an effective means of preventing future capital crimes.

At a conference in Cambridge, Massachusetts, how-ever, a group of prison officials came to the conclusion that America's prison system was a failure and that capital punishment simply did not work. They issued a statement claiming that if every inmate in the country were released from prison, the crime rate would remain about the same.

Theodore I. Kassoff, an attorney and spokesman for the group, went so far as to say, "Most people who commit crimes never get caught, and many of those who are apprehended are not incarcerated."[1]

He may have been right. At the time the United States Supreme Court announced its decision on *Furman*, some 600 persons—598 men and two women—were awaiting death in thirty-one states and the District of Columbia. These people were, in theory at least, the most violent and least likely to be rehabilitated in the nation. Yet a survey taken by the Department of Justice's Law Enforcement Assistance Administration revealed that nearly 3.2 million crimes had been committed in 1972 in five of the nation's largest cities—this despite the fact that only 1.1 million of the crimes had been reported by the police to the Federal Bureau of Investigation (FBI). The actual number of crimes committed in Philadelphia, for example, was five times greater than the number reported.

So the big question following *Furman* was, even if the death row inmates had their sentences changed to life in prison and were eventually paroled, would it really make a difference? Many critics of America's penal system were beginning to doubt it. But a large number of state legislators felt otherwise. So despite such gloomy predictions, they set about the twofold task of reviewing the convictions and sentencing of their death row inmates and revising their laws in order to make capital punishment once again legal.

There were ways to rewrite the laws so that they would withstand a test before the United States Supreme Court, of course. Even the majority of justices in *Furman* had made that clear. But how? In a case in which the majority and the minority were so deeply divided in their opinions, it was difficult to say exactly what the new laws should be.

Nonetheless, the state legislatures formed committees and hired consultants, reviewed *Furman* and other capital punishment cases, and spent hundreds—sometimes thousands—of hours in both open- and closed-door sessions. By 1975, more than two dozen states had succeeded in producing new laws, called guided discretion laws, on capital punishment. The following year, the Court upheld the capital punishment laws of all the states and declared that the death penalty in itself was not cruel or unusual punishment. This paved the way for prisons around the country to begin preparing their electric chairs and gas chambers for the 418 men and 5 women on death row since the *Furman* decision around the country. A grisly race began to see who would be the first condemned murderer to be executed in the United States since 1967.

The leading contenders for the dubious honor were Gary Mark Gilmore, thirty-five, convicted by a Utah jury of the murder of a motel night clerk, and Robert

Excell White, thirty-eight, convicted in Texas of the 1974 killing of a grocer and two customers during a robbery.

The United States Supreme Court reviewed the cases of both men and granted each of them a stay (delay) of execution. But Gilmore, convinced that he should be punished for his crime, rejected the stay. Never once showing remorse for having committed the crime, he admitted, "I feel like there was no way what happened could have been avoided. There was no other chance of choice for Mr. Bushnell [Gilmore's murder victim]. It was something that could not be stopped."[2]

True to his beliefs, Gilmore refused to cooperate in his attorney's attempts to gain an appeal. The convicted felon stated that he felt both the original trial and the sentence had been fair and that he wanted the execution to take place as soon as possible. When he learned that the American Civil Liberties Union (ACLU) was planning to file a motion for an appeal, he wrote a letter to the Court, stating that he would not cooperate in the ACLU's efforts. "These people," he said, "do not represent me."[3]

So on January 17, 1977, Gilmore left his cell for the courtyard, where he was to stand before a Utah state firing squad. Asked by the prison warden if he had any final words, Gilmore responded, "Let's do it."[4] He was put to death minutes later.

By the late 1970s, America was decidedly pro-capital punishment. National polls showed that Americans favored restoring the death penalty, lengthening prison terms, and limiting parole for criminals. Meanwhile,

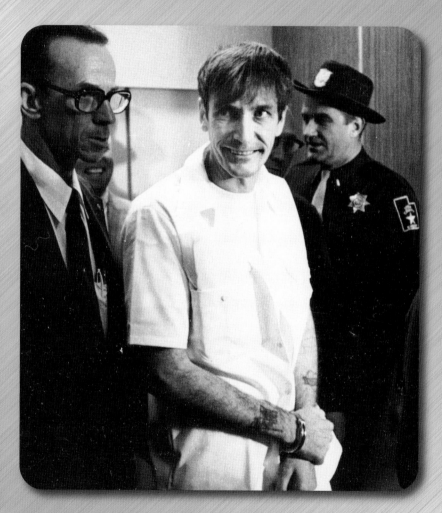

Gary Mark Gilmore was the first person executed after the death penalty was reinstated by the Supreme Court in 1976. He was executed by firing squad on January 17, 1977.

the Supreme Court approved new capital punishment laws for California, Illinois, Nebraska, North Carolina, Oklahoma, South Carolina, Tennessee, Texas, and Virginia, bringing the total number of states with such laws to thirty-five.

Yet despite public opinion, the next execution following Gilmore did not occur for nearly two-and-a-half years. John A. Spenkelink, a thirty-year-old white male, had been found guilty by a Florida court of the brutal murder of a traveling companion in a Florida motel in 1973. He was sentenced to die in the electric chair.

Unlike Gilmore, Spenkelink claimed that he had killed the man in self-defense, and he used every opportunity possible to have his conviction overturned. Legal efforts to save him were assisted by former United States Attorney General Ramsey Clark and thousands of other Americans who rallied in Spenkelink's support and against the death penalty. Following the Supreme Court's refusal to hear Spenkelink's appeal on four separate occasions, the governor of Florida ordered a clemency hearing. This hearing might have lessened the severity of his sentence. The hearing upheld the execution, and on the morning of May 25, 1979, Spenkelink was electrocuted.

That same year, on October 22, forty-six-year-old Jesse Walter Bishop was executed in a Nevada gas chamber. Bishop had confessed to eighteen murders for hire. Unlike Spenkelink, but like Gilmore, he resisted all attempts to have his case appealed, turning down offers of legal assistance from the ACLU on several occasions.

A picture of death row inmates John Spenkelink (left) and Doug McGray sits next to an anti-death penalty sign across from the Florida State Prison. Protesters rallied against the scheduled execution of John Blackwelder on May 25, 2004, the twenty-fifth anniversary of Spenkelink's electrocution.

By August 1982, thirty-seven states had enacted or revised death penalty laws that conformed to Supreme Court standards. Still, only five persons had been executed since *Furman*.

That same year, the Supreme Court ruled that the accomplice in a murder case—a man who neither planned nor directly participated in the murder—could not be executed. The ruling struck down laws in Florida and eight other states that had allowed the imposition of the death penalty for such accomplices.

The following year saw five executions in the United States—the greatest single-year number since 1965, when the nation's prisons put seven people to death. Still, only ten had been put to death since *Furman*. Part of the reason for the low number was that most of the more than one thousand men and women now on death row had been appealing their convictions. With their appeals about to run out, the nation geared up for a tremendous increase in executions. But it never came.

In 1991, 2,465 inmates awaited execution on death row. Yet only fourteen were executed. Meanwhile, the number of violent crimes in America continued to grow.

Did the return of the death penalty to America's judicial system make a marked difference in the number of capital crimes committed each year? That is a difficult—if not impossible—question to answer. FBI and other law enforcement agency statistics show that the number of capital crimes committed in America continues to rise. Whether or not it would rise at a faster rate if the threat of capital punishment were removed from our judicial system is anyone's guess. Contrary to many predictions, the crime rate did not skyrocket in the ten-year period following the banning of capital punishment in 1972. Instead, it moved only slightly up and down from the number of capital crimes committed during the year before *Furman*.

So does capital punishment have an effect on the number of capital crimes committed in America? Although many people feel capital punishment is a deterrent to serious crime, the question remains.

Another question that is equally persistent revolves around racism. Does racism still exist in America's judicial system? Many say yes. And there seems to be growing proof that they are right.

On May 13, 1981, Gary Graham, an African American, allegedly shot Bobby Lambert, a fifty-three-year-old white man, outside a Houston Safeway store. Graham was quickly apprehended, tried, and convicted of murder. But what seemed at first to be a clear-cut case of American justice in action soon turned out to be a nightmare.

Graham's conviction came to the attention of Danny Glover, the costar of the *Lethal Weapon* series of movies, and to Amnesty International, a group dedicated to helping people preserve their personal freedoms. Together they felt that Graham had not been given a fair trial. They believed that he had been convicted on too little evidence. New testimony supporting Graham's innocence, according to Glover, had been unfairly withheld from the jury. Furthermore, Glover and his

Gary Graham the week before his scheduled execution on June 22, 2000.

supporters felt that Graham was just one more example of how our legal system is bogged down in racism.

"I'm concerned about what's happening to African-American males in this country," said Glover. "I'm committed to making sure that this man receives a fair hearing."[5]

Indeed, if it had not been for Glover's commitment, Graham most likely would not be here today. "If Danny had not gotten involved," said Reverend Jew Don Boney of Houston in August 1993, "Gary would have been dead four months ago."[6]

Graham was originally convicted mostly on the testimony of one eyewitness, Bernadine Skillern, a black Houston school district clerk, who insisted that she saw Graham commit the murder. Since Graham's conviction, though, several other eyewitnesses have come forward to say that Graham could not possibly have been the murderer.

"We have six witnesses who testified the man they saw was four inches shorter than Gary [Graham]," according to Boney. "We also have five alibi witnesses who have all passed polygraphs [lie detector tests] that Gary was with them all that night."[7]

But because Texas state law prohibits new evidence from being introduced more than thirty days after a conviction, the courts had been unwilling to consider the new information.

After hearing a radio report about Graham's case in April 1993, Glover decided to get involved. "When I feel that there's been an injustice done, I get emotionally attached," said Glover.[8]

Glover traveled to Washington, D.C., where he lobbied for Graham's case. Next, he traveled to Austin, where he spoke before the Texas Legislature. Finally, in May 1993, he visited Graham in prison.

"We were able to touch hands and pray through the glass," said Glover, who described Graham as "an articulate man who's able to look at his experience from a different standpoint now."[9]

Glover never once contended that Graham was a law-abiding citizen. The son of an alcoholic father and a mentally disturbed mother, who died in 1989, Graham, like Furman, had a long history of criminal violence. He had been convicted of committing ten armed robberies in the week following Lambert's murder. One of Graham's victims, Richard Carter, was brutally attacked outside a Houston nightclub.

Still, Glover insisted that the issue in Graham's case was not the convict's character or even whether or not he actually committed the murder. "I am not carrying that burden," said Glover. "All I am asking for is a hearing."[10]

Finally, on August 3, 1993, Glover and his supporters got their wish. State District Judge Pete Lowry ordered a full hearing on the new evidence, a development that delayed Graham's execution and did not result in a reversal of his conviction.

Meanwhile, the question of racism continues to plague the supporters of capital punishment. But racism

Actor Danny Glover speaks at a press conference at a fund-raiser for Gary Graham on February 16, 1999. Graham had his execution postponed several times before finally being put to death by lethal injection in Huntsville, Texas, on June 22, 2000.

is not the only problem facing America's justice system. There are other equally disturbing problems.

Following the murder in 1986 of a clerk at a dry-cleaning store in rural Alabama, Walter McMillian, a forty-four-year-old African American, was arrested, tried, convicted, and sentenced to death. Nearly four and a half years passed before the prosecutors in the case admitted that McMillian was not guilty. The state was planning to execute an innocent man.

The thought of wrongfully putting someone to death for a crime he or she did not commit has concerned both pro- and anti-capital punishment forces for decades. Advocates of the death penalty insist that wrongful death cases are rare. Challengers to the death penalty say that no one knows for sure how many innocent people have been wrongly put to death over the years. Even one, they insist, is too many.

McMillian, fifty-one, was finally freed March 2, 1993, after Monroe County District Attorney Tommy Chapman admitted that McMillian had spent nearly six years on death row for a crime he did not commit. By that time, all three of the prosecution's main witnesses in the case had admitted that they had lied when pointing to McMillian as the murderer. A state appeals court ruled that McMillian was entitled to a new trial because the state prosecutors had withheld evidence that would have been helpful in McMillian's defense.

Chapman, who did not become district attorney until 1990, more than two years after McMillian's trial, admitted that the prosecution of the McMillian case had been mishandled from the start. But he insisted there was no evidence that there had been a deliberate attempt to pin the murder on anyone.

"A lot of things just didn't add up," according to Chapman, "and a lot of other things weren't looked into. You can certainly argue that there was some carelessness involved [in the prosecution's handling of the case], but there's no evidence that anybody tried to put [McMillian] on death row for something he didn't do."[11]

The former district attorney who prosecuted the McMillian case, Ted Pearson, said that convicting an innocent man of murder was "the last thing" he would ever do. "All I did is put the evidence I had in front of a jury. It was their decision to convict him, not mine."[12]

Other state prosecutors involved with the case admitted that it was a mistake from the very beginning. But they said that McMillian's eventual release from prison is proof that America's justice system works. They gave credit to Chapman for working so hard to see that McMillian went free.

"The only reason he's not still . . . waiting to go on trial again today is because the state and its agents recognized a problem and did something about it," according to Chapman.[13]

Marvin White, Jr., an assistant attorney general whose job is to defend death-penalty appeals in the neighboring state of Mississippi, agreed. "The wheels of justice may grind slowly, but they do grind fine," he said.[14] Jane Byers, an assistant attorney general in North Carolina, defended the Alabama prosecution's handling of the McMillian case. Once they learned that McMillian was innocent, she said, they did everything they could to free him. "That's the way [the system is] supposed to work."[15]

Still, McMillian's defense attorneys believed that the case proves just how flawed the justice system is. It was too easy to convict their client of a murder he did not commit, and it was too hard to free him once the truth became known, even though the evidence of McMillian's innocence was overwhelming.

"This case is unusual only in the sense that McMillian's innocence was so demonstrable and relatively obvious," according to Bryan Stevenson of the Alabama Capital Representation Resource Center, the group that handled McMillian's appeal. "What's outrageous about it is the deliberate indifference to his plight."[16]

Stevenson's co-counsel, Michael O'Connor, added, "They [the prosecutors] fought us tooth and nail every step of the way. And they even had the nerve to suggest that we be [reprimanded] for bringing this appeal."[17]

McMillian's attorneys insisted that race was a large factor in McMillian's trial. McMillian was dating a white woman at the time of his arrest.

"From the comments made at the time of his arrest [by the arresting officers], there's no question that [they felt that] any black man who was bold enough to have a relationship with a white woman was considered dangerous enough to commit a murder," said Stevenson.[18]

To make matters worse, McMillian's trial was moved to a neighboring county made up mostly of whites. Only one black was included on the jury, and the prosecutor at one point asked a witness to describe McMillian's white girlfriend in an effort to turn the jury against the defendant.

In the end, McMillian was convicted on the testimony of three men. One swore under oath that he had driven McMillian to the cleaners and witnessed the murder. The other two said that they had seen McMillian's truck, which they described as a "lowrider," near the cleaners at the time of the assault.

Even though the defense called seven witnesses who testified that he had been home when the murder occurred, the jury found McMillian guilty and recommended that he receive life in prison. But the judge, who was also white, sentenced him to death.

Over the next several months, McMillian's requests for appeal were denied twice by the courts, even after the defense had proven that all three of the state's witnesses had received favorable treatment or a share of the reward money in exchange for their testimony.

Finally, with the evidence mounting against them, the state could no longer ignore the facts. McMillian's attorneys pointed out that the defendant's truck had not been converted into a lowrider until more than six months after the murder had been committed. And the man who had testified that he had driven McMillian to the dry-cleaning store admitted that he had made up his story under pressure from the police.

Following the reversal of his conviction, McMillian found himself trying to put his life back in order. He left Alabama on a brief trip and considered moving away permanently, but he realized that he did not have anywhere better to go.

"The same thing could've happened anywhere," he said.[19] And he was probably right.

Such miscarriages of justice happen rarely, but their occurrences are enough to generate regular calls for judicial reform. Meanwhile, the Supreme Court, forced to walk a thin line between supporting the right of individual states to impose the death penalty and ruling the death penalty unconstitutional, seems to be more confused than ever about which side to take.

In *Furman* v. *Georgia* (1972), the Court had ruled that capital punishment that took place "freakishly" was unconstitutional. In *Gregg* v. *Georgia* (1976), it went one step further in saying that the death penalty was constitutional when imposed fairly and with impartial discretion. In doing so, Justice Potter Stewart acknowledged that the death penalty could serve a legitimate purpose in deterring crime.

Between 1976 and 1982, the Court asserted its authority in upholding the fair administration of capital justice. During that six-year period, it decided fifteen capital cases. In all but one, it reversed the death sentence that the state had imposed.

More recently, the Supreme Court has weakened in its resolve to restrict the death penalty. In *Stanford* v. *Kentucky* (1989), the Court ruled that a state can execute persons as young as sixteen. In *Penry* v. *Lynaugh* (1989), it ruled that a state can execute mentally retarded persons. In *McCleskey* v. *Kemp* (1987), it ruled that a state could execute persons even if they have suffered racial discrimination.

So while the questions revolving around the constitutionality of capital punishment rage on, the two sides—including the justices themselves—continue to jockey for position. Retired justice Lewis Powell has suggested that the time may be right for Congress to end such a "haphazard" practice as capital punishment.[20]

On the other hand, it seems as though that may not be Congress's responsibility, but rather that of the Supreme Court itself. After all, it is the Court's role to see that capital punishment is imposed "fairly, and with reasonable consistency, or not at all" (*Eddings* v. *Oklahoma*, 1982).[21]

In any event, one thing is clear. *Furman* v. *Georgia* helped change—for a while, at least—the racial cross section of convicted murderers executed in the United States. While most inmates executed prior to *Furman* had been black, seven out of the first eight following *Furman* and the reinstatement of the death penalty were white.

Could it be that the states, anxious to avoid another run-in with the United States Supreme Court and not wanting to risk losing forever their right to execute convicted felons, deliberately selected white inmates? Could it be that in their efforts to silence the cries of discrimination from the civil rights groups that had hounded them since *Furman*, they overreacted in their selection of inmates to execute? This is one possibility. Another is simply that the nation's judicial system finally caught up with the rest of America, and that Americans—long since grown tired of rampant crime, regardless of race—had had enough.

That is something we may never know—or at least not until another challenge to the death penalty is placed before the Supreme Court.

In the meantime, one thing is clear. Capital crimes in America are being committed at a record-breaking pace, while our prisons are overflowing with convicted felons awaiting sentencing and execution. Equally clear is that while the case of *Furman* v. *Georgia* has had a major impact on capital punishment in America, no one yet knows exactly where the question of capital punishment will take us.

The Passage of Time

CHAPTER

8

More than six hundred death row inmates who had been sentenced to death between 1967 and 1972 found their sentences suddenly lifted as a result of the U. S. Supreme Court's ruling in *Furman* v. *Georgia*,[1] but before long, the number of inmates on death row began to climb again as the states set about revising their laws in order to meet the new requirements of the post–*Furman* Court.

Once the Burger Court had rendered its groundbreaking decision on the constitutionality of capital punishment, it was immediately faced with a new task. The Court had to take upon itself the monumental project of reviewing all individual state laws providing for capital punishment. It was clear to everyone from *Furman* that the Court had found Georgia's death penalty laws unconstitutional, but what about those of New York and Alabama and Oklahoma and all of the other states that had similar laws on their books? Would those laws also fail to meet the Court's constitutionality test . . . or would they somehow be upheld as valid?

The capital punishment laws that had been passed by the state legislatures at the time fell mainly into two broad groups. The first group consisted of guided discretion laws, which were quickly found by the Court to be constitutional. The other group consisted of mandatory death penalty laws, which the Court equally decisively struck down as unconstitutional.

The Court upheld the guided discretion laws in three cases related to *Furman*. These included *Gregg* v. *Georgia*, 428 U.S. 153 (1976), *Jurek* v. *Texas*, 428 U.S. 262 (1976), and *Proffitt* v. *Florida*, 428 U.S. 242 (1976). In all three cases, the Georgia, Texas, and Florida laws upheld by the Supreme Court consisted of two component parts, or stages. In the first stage, they granted the states' sentencing courts the discretion to impose the death sentence for specific crimes, which the states had long done in the past.

But the three states went further than that by providing for a second stage in a two-part, or bifurcated, trial in which the first stage of the capital trial was held to decide a defendant's guilt or innocence, while the second stage determined the sentence of the guilty party after taking into consideration any aggravating or mitigating factors. In Georgia and Texas, the jury decided the final sentence; in Florida, the judge made the decision.

The state laws that the Court struck down, on the other hand, were known as mandatory death penalty laws. They provided the death penalty for committing specific crimes without taking into consideration a second sentencing stage to provide for a judge or a jury consideration of mitigating factors before pronouncing sentence. The Court declared these mandatory death penalty laws unconstitutional in *Woodson* v. *North Carolina*, 428 U.S. 280 (1976), and *Roberts* v. *Louisiana*, 428 U.S. 325 (1976).

The Supreme Court's rulings on these capital punishment cases led to striking down the mandatory death penalty laws that existed in twenty-one states, which, in turn, resulted in commuting the sentences of hundreds of offenders who had been sentenced either to life imprisonment or death.[2]

The Court After *Furman*

After the Supreme Court had decided that capital punishment was not unconstitutional and reinstated the death penalty under its new guidelines, it found that its work in the arena of capital punishment was far from over. In fact, it had only begun. New capital punishment challenges confronted the Court almost immediately. The Court would have to be the ultimate arbiter on which state statutes passed the test of constitutionality and which did not. Sometimes the Court upheld state law; other times, it did not.

In *Coker* v. *Georgia*, 433 U.S. 584 (1977), the Supreme Court ruled that applying the death penalty in rape cases was unconstitutional because the sentence did not fit the crime. As a result of the ruling, twenty inmates, three white and seventeen black, sentenced to death on rape convictions were removed from death rows throughout the United States. Although the Court's decision did not immediately extend to the rape of children, it is expected to consider that matter shortly.

In 1978's *Lockett* v. *Ohio*, 438 U.S. 586, the Court ruled that every possible mitigating factor to the crime must be considered. Ohio had limited the mitigating factors that could be taken into account to a specific list. Such actions by Ohio, the Court decided, were selective and arbitrary and thus did not meet constitutional requirements.

Following the 1976 *Gregg* decision upholding the constitutionality of Georgia's death penalty law following *Furman*, nearly three-quarters of the states reinstated capital punishment in their statutes, the most recent state being New York in 1995.[3] However, the high court in New York struck down its capital punishment law as being unconstitutional in 2004.[4]

As of March 2009, then, thirty-five states and the federal government have capital punishment laws. The fifteen states that do not have death penalty laws are Alaska, Hawaii, Iowa, Maine, Massachusetts, Michigan, Minnesota, New Jersey, New Mexico, New York, North Dakota, Rhode Island, Vermont, West Virginia, and Wisconsin, along with the District of Columbia.

An anti-death penalty demonstration takes place outside the Supreme Court Building in Washington, D.C., on June 30, 2006, thirty years after *Gregg* v. *Georgia*. In the *Gregg* decision, the Court reinstated the death penalty in Georgia four years after *Furman* v. *Georgia* deemed it unconstitutional.

Court Cases Post-*Furman*

The U.S. Supreme Court has heard several important cases since it struck down Georgia's death penalty statutes in *Furman*. In one effort to assure that capital punishments laws are applied equally throughout the nation, the Court, in another Georgia test, *Godfrey* v. *Georgia*, 446 U.S. 420 (1980), sent back for retrial several cases on grounds that the application of the provision calling for the death penalty were too broad and overly vague. The Georgia legislature had decided that if an offense was "outrageously or wantonly vile, horrible, or inhumane, in that it involved torture, depravity of mind, or an aggravated battery to the victim," the death penalty was warranted.

The Court ruled to the contrary, stating that while its ruling did not affect the state's right to embrace the death penalty, it found that the relevant facts in *Godfrey* were not substantially different from those in other cases in which that same Georgia state legislative provision was not applied.

In *Beck* v. *Alabama*, 447 U.S. 625 (1980), the Court struck a portion of Alabama's death penalty law that prevented juries from convicting defendants of an included lesser offense rather than of the capital crime itself. It was an all-or-nothing approach that the Court saw as a means of Alabama coercing its juries into convicting the accused of a capital crime rather than letting him walk free on a lesser conviction. Until the Supreme Court had overruled the law, Alabama juries were required either to convict a defendant of the capital crime charges brought against him or to acquit him of all crimes.

In yet another decision a few years later, the Court ventured into the territory of civil rights when it ruled in *Ford* v. *Wainwright*, 477 U.S. 399 (1986), that executing a person judged to be insane is unconstitutional. Similarly, it ruled in *Thompson* v. *Oklahoma*, 487 U.S. 815 (1988), that youths below sixteen years of age at the time of their offenses cannot be executed.

Death Penalty Statistics

Since its 1993 finding in *Eddings* v. *Oklahoma* that capital punishment be imposed "fairly, and with reasonable consistency, or not at all,"[5] the United States has seen at least ten executions a year. There were seventy-four executions in 1997. From 1977 to 2007, a total of 1,099 executions took place.[6] Of the executed prisoners during 2008, twenty were white and seventeen were black. All thirty-seven executed inmates were male.[7]

By the end of 1997, thirty-six states and the federal government had enacted capital punishment laws. As of 2009, fifteen states have no death penalty. By the end of 1996, 3,242 prisoners were under sentence of death. All had been convicted of murder.[8]

In the more than thirty-five years since the Court overturned the state of Georgia's death penalty with *Furman*, it has struggled to oversee and clarify the constitutionality of all capital punishment laws. During that time, statistics show that the number of inmates on

Number of Executions in the United States, 1930–2008

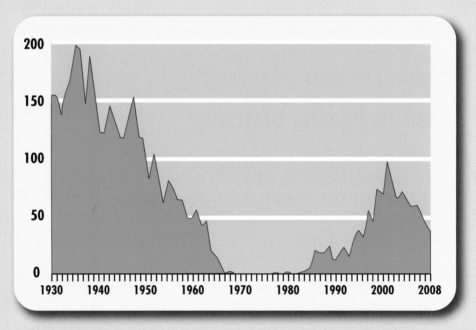

Source: Bureau of Justice Statistics

This chart shows the number of executions that took place in the United States between 1930 and 2008. One can clearly see how the nation's view of capital punishment changed throughout the years. The 1930s and 1940s were obviously pro-death penalty with more than one hundred executions occurring every year from 1930 to 1949. The numbers dropped during the 1950s and 1960s. No one was executed between 1968 and 1976. The trend changed once again with a dramatic increase in persons being put to death during the 1990s and 2000s, reaching a peak of 98 executions in 1999.

Number of Prisoners on Death Row by Race, 1968–2007

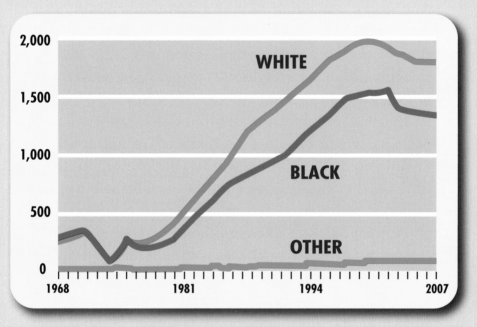

Source: Bureau of Justice Statistics

This line chart shows the number of persons sentenced to death by race from 1968 to 2007. There were more African Americans on death row than whites up until the Supreme Court reinstated the death penalty in 1976. Since then, the majority of prisoners awaiting execution have been white.

death row are no longer predominantly black but more in keeping with overall U.S. Census Bureau statistical data.

In 2007, for example, the total number of white inmates awaiting execution nationwide was 1,804. For blacks, the number was 1,345, with other races accounting for a total of 71.[9] Those figures contrast sharply to 1968, where whites accounted for 243 death row inmates, blacks totaled 271 awaiting execution, and other races tallied three.[10]

If it has accomplished nothing else, the Court, in defining which laws are and which are not constitutionally equitable, has overturned the skewed national statistics that once existed and has since helped to apply capital punishment laws somewhat more equally.

A much stickier question, however, remains. Does capital punishment work? Does the threat of putting a convicted felon to death in response to his criminal activities offer an effective deterrent to crime? The answer to that question is not so clear-cut. Some people insist that it does; others say no.

The Court may never be able to answer that question adequately; nor, according to most Court watchers and constitutional analysts, should it.

The role of the U.S. Supreme Court in deciding the future of capital punishment in America is not to help to determine whether or not capital punishment is effective. That job falls into the hands of our legislators and their constituents—the voters across the land.

Clarence Brandley was charged with murder and sentenced to death in 1981 but was exonerated in 1990. He and other former death row inmates gather for a news conference in Austin, Texas, on October 31, 2008, asking for a moratorium on executions in the state. Many wrongfully convicted prisoners have been released due to new evidence coming to light. However, no one knows how many innocent lives have been and will be lost in the death chambers of the nation's prisons.

Rather, the role of the Court in capital punishment is to see that so long as capital punishment is constitutional, the states apply the death penalty laws equally, without prejudice, malice, or special consideration.

Beginning with William Furman and the groundbreaking case of *Furman* v. *Georgia*, the Court has done just that. It established itself in the role of primary constitutional arbiter in that capital punishment case and has been continuing in its ever-evolving role ever since.

But the question remains: will the United States, with or without the blessings of the Supreme Court, and with or without conclusive evidence that the death penalty plays a significant role in reducing the incidence of serious crime, ever ban capital punishment?

That is a question the U.S. Supreme Court cannot possibly answer. For that, only the passage of time and the will of the nation's people will tell.

Chapter Notes

CHAPTER 1. Georgia, 1967

1. Maureen Harrison and Steve Gilbert, eds., *Landmark Decisions of the United States Supreme Court II* (Beverly Hills, Calif.: Excellent Books, 1992), p. 125.

CHAPTER 2. Capital Punishment in America

1. "U.S. Executions Since 1976," *Clark County Prosecuting Attorney*, 2009, < http://www.clarkprosecutor.org/html/death/usexecute .htm > (March 23, 2009).

CHAPTER 3. A Case for Furman

1. *Trop* v. *Dulles*, 356 U.S. 86 (1958).
2. William Sharp McKechnie, *Magna Carta: A Commentary on the Great Chapter of King John* (New York: Burt Franklin, 1914), p. 287.
3. Ibid., p. 284.
4. Maureen Harrison and Steve Gilbert, eds., *Landmark Decisions of the United States Supreme Court II* (Beverly Hills, Calif.: Excellent Books, 1992), pp. 119–120.
5. *McGautha* v. *California*, 402 U.S. 183 (1971).
6. Ibid.
7. *Furman* v. *Georgia*, 408 U.S. 238 (1972).

CHAPTER 4. A Case for the State of Georgia

1. *Wilkerson* v. *Utah*, 99 U.S 130 (1878).
2. *In re Kemmler*, 136 U.S. 436 (1890).
3. Syllabus Opinion, Supreme Court of Georgia, April 24, 1969.
4. Ibid.
5. Ibid.
6. Ibid.
7. Ibid.
8. Ibid.

CHAPTER 5. To the Highest Court

1. The Oyez Project, *Furman* v. *Georgia*, 408 U.S. 238 (1972), *The Oyez Project*, n.d., < http://www.oyez.org/cases/1970-1979/1971/1971_69_5003/ > (February 22, 2009).
2. Ibid.
3. Ibid.
4. Ibid.
5. Ibid.
6. Ibid.
7. Ibid.
8. Ibid.
9. Ibid.
10. Ibid.
11. Abraham L. Davis and Barbara Luck Graham, *The Supreme Court, Race, and Civil Rights* (Thousand Oaks, Calif.: Sage Publications, Inc., 1995), p. 99.
12. The Oyez Project, *Furman* v. *Georgia*, 408 U.S. 238 (1972).
13. Ibid.
14. Ibid.
15. Ibid.
16. Ibid.

CHAPTER 6. The Decision

1. *Furman* v. *Georgia*, 408 U.S. 238 (1972).
2. Ibid.
3. Ibid.
4. Ibid.
5. Ibid.
6. Ibid.
7. Ibid.

Chapter Notes

CHAPTER 7. Yesterday, Today, and Tomorrow

1. *Funk and Wagnalls Standard Reference Encyclopedia Yearbook* (New York: Funk and Wagnalls, 1972), p. 170.
2. Robert W. Jolly, Jr., and Edward Sagarin, "The First Eight After Furman: Who Was Executed With the Return of the Death Penalty?" *Crime and Delinquency*, vol. 30, no. 4, October 1984, p. 612.
3. Ibid., p. 613.
4. Ibid.
5. Susan Shindehette, Lois Armstrong, and Anne Maier, "Death Row Rescue?" *People Weekly*, vol. 40, no. 7, August 16, 1993, p. 53.
6. Ibid.
7. Ibid.
8. Ibid., p. 54
9. Ibid.
10. Ibid.
11. Mark Hansen, "The Murder Case That Unraveled," *ABA Journal*, June 1993, p. 30.
12. Ibid.
13. Ibid.
14. Ibid.
15. Ibid.
16. Ibid.
17. Ibid.
18. Ibid.
19. Ibid., p. 31.
20. Cornelius F. Murphy, "The Supreme Court and Capital Punishment: A New Hands-Off Approach," *USA Today*, March 1993, p. 52.
21. Ibid.

CHAPTER 8. The Passage of Time

1. Melissa S. Green, "History of the Death Penalty and Recent Developments," *Focus on the Death Penalty*, May 2, 2005, Justice Center, University of Alaska Anchorage, January 29, 2009, < http://justice.uaa.alaska.edu/death/history.html > (March 23, 2009).
2. Ibid.
3. Ibid.
4. "The Death Penalty: Questions and Answers," *American Civil Liberties Union* (ACLU), April 9, 2007, < http://www.aclu.org/capital/facts/10534res20070409.html > (April 15, 2009).
5. Cornelius F. Murphy, "The Supreme Court and Capital Punishment: A New Hands-Off Approach," *USA Today*, March 1993, p. 52.
6. U.S. Department of Justice, "Capital Punishment Statistics," *Bureau of Justice Statistics*, January 23, 2009, < http://www.ojp.usdoj.gov/bjs/cp.htm > (March 23, 2009).
7. Ibid.
8. "Prisoners on Death Row by Race," *Bureau of Justice Statistics*, December 4, 2008, < http://www.ojp.usdoj.gov/bjs/glance/tables/drracetab.htm > (March 23, 2009).
9. Ibid.
10. Ibid.

Glossary

admissibility—The condition of being allowed as legal evidence in a court proceeding.

amendment—A change to an existing agreement or rule.

Bill of Rights—The first ten amendments to the United States constitution.

bill—A proposal that could become a law if it is passed by the House of Representatives and the Senate and is signed by the president.

certiorari—A legal document issued by a superior court to an inferior court.

civil rights—Rights that protect citizens from unjust government interference and ensure their political participation without discrimination.

concurring opinion—An opinion written by a judge or judges who agree with the majority opinion but hold a different reason for their view(s).

contention—A point that is maintained in a legal proceeding.

dissenting opinion—An opinion written by a judge or judges who disagree with the majority opinion.

evidence—Something that is offered up as proof during a legal proceeding.

federal—Having to do with the central (national) form of government, as opposed to a state or local government.

majority opinion—A ruling supported by the majority of judges in a case.

petition—A formal, official request.

precedent—Prior legal decisions that establish a foundation for future decisions.

repeal—To nullify or remove.

unconstitutional law—A law that the Supreme Court declares a violation of either the U. S. constitution or state constitution.

United States Constitution—The basic law forming the U. S. government. It consists of seven articles and twenty-seven amendments.

United States Supreme Court—A judicial body comprised of nine justices. As the highest court in the U. S., it holds final say over whether or not a law is constitutional.

Further Reading

Elster, Jean Alicia, ed. *The Death Penalty.* Detroit, Mich.: Greenhaven Press, 2005.

Gershman, Gary P. *Death Penalty on Trial: A Handbook With Cases, Laws, and Documents.* Santa Barbara, Calif.: ABC-CLIO, 2005.

Roensch, Greg. *Furman v. Georgia: Cruel and Unusual Punishment.* New York: Chelsea House, 2007.

Stefoff, Rebecca. *Furman v. Georgia: Debating the Death Penalty.* New York: Benchmark Press, 2007.

Internet Addresses

"Furman v. Georgia," The Oyez Project
http://www.oyez.org/cases/1970-1979/1971/1971_69_5003/

"Furman v. Georgia," University of Missouri
http://www.law.umkc.edu/faculty/projects/ftrials/conlaw/furman.html

Constitutional Rights Foundation
http://www.crf-usa.org/

Charters of Freedom: The Declaration of Independence, The Constitution, The Bill of Rights
http://www.archives.gov/exhibits/charters/charters.html

Index

Index